I Am a Confident King

I Am a Confident King
Text copyright © 2015 by Jasmine Furr
Illustrations Copyright © 2015 by (Jasmine Furr)
Manufactured in the United States of America

All rights reserved. No part of this book may be used or reproduced in any capacity without written permission except in the case of brief quotations intended for use in critical articles and reviews. For more information address Untraditional Publishing Company, LLC.

JFurrBooks.com

ISBN 978-0-9887775-5-2

I Am a Confident King

By
Jasmine Furr

Foreward

In many ways, Jamaican-born political revolutionary Marcus Garvey was a king. He embodied the necessary self-assurance and audacity to project himself publicly as a worthy leader. Garvey's feather-adorned regalia perfectly accented his persona, while the businesses, organizations, and publications he developed for the uplift of Black people around the world authenticated it. His global influence, in large part, can be attributed to how he felt about himself, which allowed others who witnessed his glory to feel at least a portion of that same greatness in themselves. Garvey declared, "If you haven't confidence in yourself, you are twice defeated in the race of life. With confidence, you have won even before you have started."

I Am a Confident King works to instill a winning self-worth at an early age. The language empowers young readers to not only see and speak words of affirmation about themselves, but also to visualize themselves as agents in their own destinies in a practical way. From achieving in school and enjoying positive interactions with friends to making healthy food choices, the journey this book captures is simple, yet powerfully meaningful. The message of believing in oneself is one both parents and children will appreciate.

There is no time more imperative than now to provide our Black male youth with positive support and constructive images. As an educator, I often share, "Limits on our potential evaporate when we can look in the mirror and like what we see." I Am a Confident King effectively assists this mission and allows our precious children to view a reflection of themselves on its pages and love what they see.

Enjoy,
Dr. Kimberly Brown
Assistant Professor of History, Alabama State University
And Author of Queen Like Me: The True Story of Girls Who Changed The World and
Superhero Like Me: The True Story of Champions Who Changed The World

This book belongs to

_____

and is dedicated to all the Kings!

The words made him feel like he could do anything!
He went to class and he paid attention easily,
his hand was raised in every class,
he knew the answers to what the teachers asked,
and in group activities, he did his part.
"I do this," he said,

"because I am smart!"

he said. "Away from her, you must go," and soon enough, what do you know! The bullies walked away, and the girl was safe "because," King said, "I am brave!"

During recess, King had so much fun playing around; even on his own, he climbed trees, ran through the grass, jumped around, and had lots of laughs. He said, "I am so much fun! I like being me, and I can say, I am happy!"

Then King walked to his grandmother's house with smiles and love all around. He was surrounded by good food with family visiting in the living room. King shouted with joy, "I love my family! I can say, *I am Happy!*"

*King is smart, brave, happy, and great,
and so am I!*

*There are other words to describe me
that I can write!*

Directions: Below, write other words that describe you!

_____

_____

_____

_____

_____

_____

_____

_____

_____

Directions: Write in the "I AM" sentence and draw what the word means to you!

I am smart.

I am brave

I am happy

I am great

"Young Black Man, you can
Young Black Man, you will
Young Black Men are skilled
Young Black Men, be bold
because Black is gold"

Londrelle
theRunForJustice.org
Author of Justice for All

You are great, young child

*You are great, young child
like every little Queen and King
you can go anywhere
you can do anything*

*Tell yourself you can
believe that you will
know that every dream
can be real*

*Say
I am smart
I am brave
I am happy
I am great
and today
can be a perfect day*

*Your words will become actions
your actions will make them true
you will be great
in whatever you want to do
your words will take you
wherever you want to go
you are great, young child
just tell yourself so*

-Jasmine Furr

Jasmine Furr is an author, speaker, and poet who is always quick to smile. With her company, Untraditional Publishing Company, LLC, her purpose is the encourage people to love and accept themselves.

Jasmine was born in Atlanta, GA to Minga and Johnny Furr. She grew up in the city of St. Louis, MO with her parents and grandparents all under one roof. She made her first stage appearance and publication in 2007, while attending Florida A. and M. University. In 2011, she started Untraditional Publishing Company, LLC, a company focused on creating opportunities for new and first-time authors with a positive message.

Her breakout book, In Full Bloom: a collection of poems by Jasmine Furr, has over 100 poems on faith, family, love, culture, and self. In Full Bloom has been featured in many different outlets. The St. Louis American featured her poem Anniversary. The book landed a feature on Essence.com and the popular webseries Quarter Century from her poem Quarter Life Crisis. In Full Bloom was also featured in the Authors Pavilion at the 2014 Congressional Black Caucus Annual Legislative Conference (CBCALC). During the CBCALC, Jasmine was introduced as "our next Maya Angelou". Appreciating all aspects of life, In Full Bloom allows all of us to live our lives to the fullest.

In the wake of the Black Lives Matter movement, Jasmine launched Dear Black Twitter: poems of the young black experience. The book was featured on the Huffington Post, at the AARLC Annual Black Empowerment Summit, at the 3 Kings Lecture, on the R.I.Z.E. African-American Read-In, as well as various Instagram accounts: Books for the Soul, the Black Book List, Afrikan Library, African Unification, Ujamaa Box, and more. This is an empowerment book that takes on the best of our identity, love, and solidarity.

Jasmine is available as a speaker, publisher, vendor, and performer for any age group. Feel free to contact her:
Email: Untraditionalllc@gmail.com
Instagram/Twitter: Jasmine_Furr
Facebook: Jasmine Furr
website: JFurrBooks.com

Order your copy of In Full Bloom and Dear Black Twitter on JFurrBooks.com or Amazon.com

www.ingramcontent.com/pod-product-compliance
Lightning Source LLC
Chambersburg PA
CBHW041120300426
44112CB00002B/39